Wealth begins when you stop chasing money and start mastering it.

UNLOCK WEALTH

TJ HILL

Published by TJ HILL
Paperback ISBN: 979-8-9941394-2-4
Special Edition
Printed in the United States of America
For information, permissions, or inquiries, contact:
www.tjhillbooks.com

Book Cover by SK Lynne

If prosperity is a way of thinking, wealth is a series of decisions.

Unlock Wealth is a hands-on workbook that helps you turn insight into structure, goals into plans, and intention into measurable progress.

INTRODUCTION

Thank you for purchasing this journal. It was created to help you rethink your relationship with money, manage your finances, and take control of your financial life. I'm going to take you on a journey toward clarity, confidence, and power. This journal pairs well with *The Power to Prosperity*, but it also stands strong on its own. I'm excited to share it with you.

Grab your favorite pen.

Find a place to relax and focus.

Take three deep breaths.

And let's get started.

WHAT IS PROSPERITY?

Prosperity is a multifaceted concept that encompasses more than just material wealth. At its core, prosperity embodies a state of well-being and abundance, where individuals and societies thrive in various aspects of life. Beyond financial success, prosperity includes elements such as good health, fulfilling relationships, personal growth, and a sense of purpose.

When we think of prosperity, it's essential to recognize that it goes beyond the accumulation of possessions. While financial stability can contribute to a comfortable life, *true* prosperity lies in finding balance and contentment in both material and non-material aspects. This delicate equilibrium allows individuals to experience a deeper sense of fulfillment and happiness.

In a prosperous society, there is a collective effort to uplift everyone, ensuring that opportunities are accessible to all, regardless of their background or circumstances. Education and healthcare systems play a crucial role in empowering individuals to reach their full potential, fostering a more equitable and prosperous community.

Moreover, prosperity thrives on innovation and creativity. A society that encourages and supports entrepreneurship, scientific advancements, and artistic expression is more likely to prosper. These endeavors not only boost economic growth but also enrich the cultural fabric of the community, nurturing a vibrant and thriving environment.

Deliberately adopting a soft internal tone of voice allows for introspection and contemplation, leading to a deeper understanding of the topic. It's through this gentle approach that we can explore the idea that prosperity isn't merely about the accumulation of wealth but a profound sense of well-being and fulfillment that transcends monetary gains.

In conclusion, prosperity is a harmonious blend of material abundance, emotional well-being, social cohesion, and intellectual growth. It is the realization of human potential and the celebration of diversity. Embracing a holistic perspective of prosperity can pave the way for a more compassionate and sustainable future, where everyone can flourish and contribute to the betterment of society.

THE IMPORTANCE OF DEFINING YOUR PERSONAL DEFINITION OF PROSPERITY AND FINANCIAL FREEDOM.

Defining your personal definition of prosperity and financial freedom is an essential step towards achieving a fulfilling and meaningful life. By crafting a clear vision of what these concepts mean to you, you set the stage for purpose-driven actions and a more intentional approach to your financial decisions.

Prosperity, beyond its conventional understanding, is deeply subjective. It means different things to different people. For some, it might involve having a successful career, a loving family, and good health, while for others, it could be about pursuing personal passions, contributing to their community, or experiencing spiritual growth. Defining prosperity on your terms empowers you to focus on what truly matters to you, rather than conforming to societal norms or external expectations.

Similarly, financial freedom is more than just a numerical value in a bank account. It encompasses the ability to make choices that align with your values and aspirations without being hindered by financial constraints. This could include the freedom to pursue your dream job, start a business, travel the world, or give back to causes you care about. By having a personalized understanding of financial freedom, you gain clarity on your financial goals and the steps needed to achieve them.

Crafting your definition of prosperity and financial freedom enables you to set meaningful and achievable objectives. It provides you with a sense of direction and motivation, making it easier to stay focused on your journey.

Moreover, a clear vision helps you make informed financial decisions, as you can assess whether your choices align with your values and long-term aspirations.

Another crucial aspect of defining your personal vision of prosperity and financial freedom is that it fosters a healthy relationship with money. Rather than viewing money as an end, you start seeing it as a tool to support your life goals and enhance your overall well-being. This shift in perspective often leads to more
responsible financial behaviors, such as saving, investing, and managing debt wisely.

Furthermore, understanding your personal definition of prosperity and financial freedom can provide a sense of contentment and gratitude. When you acknowledge the aspects of your life that truly matter to you, you begin to appreciate the abundance already present, which may not always be monetary. This gratitude mindset can contribute to a positive outlook on life, reducing stress and enhancing overall happiness.

In conclusion, defining your personal definition of prosperity and financial freedom is a crucial step towards leading a purposeful and fulfilled life. It empowers you to focus on what truly matters to you, align your financial decisions with your values, and cultivate a healthier relationship with money. By envisioning prosperity and financial freedom on your terms, you embark on a journey of self-discovery and intentional living, leading to a more meaningful and enriching existence.

Take a moment to reflect before you write. Be specific, be honest, and resist the urge to minimize what you want.

Date:______________________________

How do *you* define prosperity?

____

____

What does financial freedom mean to you?

____

____

Write the exact dollar amount you want.

____

How do you plan to pursue this money?

____

____

Why do you deserve wealth, beyond survival or security?

____

____

SETTING CLEAR FINANCIAL GOALS TO ACHIEVE PROSPERITY AND FINANCIAL FREEDOM AND HOW TO DO IT

Setting clear financial goals is a pivotal step on the path to achieving prosperity and financial freedom. By defining specific, measurable, achievable, relevant, and time-bound objectives, you can gain clarity, direction, and motivation to manage their finances effectively. This guide will explore the significance of setting clear financial goals, the key elements of goals, and practical strategies to implement them.

The Importance of Setting Clear Financial Goals:

1. *Clarity and Focus*: Clear financial goals provide a sense of direction and purpose. They help you understand what they want to achieve and prioritize their actions accordingly. With a well-defined road map, it becomes easier to stay focused on the journey towards prosperity and financial freedom. Write your goals below.

GOALS

1.____

2.____

3.____

4.____

5.____

2. *Motivation and Commitment*: Having specific goals ignites motivation and commitment. When individuals can envision the rewards of achieving their objectives, they are more likely to persist in their efforts, even during challenging times.

What is your purpose?

____

____

What are you doing this for?

____

____

3. *Financial Discipline*: Setting clear financial goals encourages disciplined money management. It fosters responsible spending, saving, and investing behaviors, as every financial decision is aligned with the overarching objectives.

How much can I save per month: _________________

Where can I invest my saved money?

 If you need guidance on this, please speak to a professional investment advisor. Even if you only have a few hundred dollars to your name. It is never too early to start investing that towards your future.

4. *Measurement of Progress:* With defined goals, you can track their progress and adjust as needed. Regularly reviewing the advancement towards their financial aspirations helps identify areas for improvement and keeps them accountable.

Please read your goals and plan every day and when you feel the need to adjust; make sure you put the date the adjustment was made.

Adjustment dates: ______________________________________

____

5. *Empowerment and Confidence*: Successfully reaching financial goals boosts confidence and empowers you to take charge of their financial future. It instills a sense of accomplishment and a belief in one's ability to make sound financial choices.

Please write five affirmations to enlighten your confidence and power:

____

____

____

____

____

KEY ELEMENTS OF FINANCIAL GOALS

1. *Specific*: The goals should be clearly defined and unambiguous. Instead of vague objectives like "save more money," a specific goal could be "save $10,000 for an emergency fund in the next 12 months."

Using the goals you listed previously, write five *specific* goals that support and move you toward them:

GOALS

1. ____

2. ____

3. ____

4. ____

5. ____

2. *Measurable*: Goals should be quantifiable, allowing you to track progress. Measurable goals help answer questions like "How much?" or "How many?" in relation to the target.

How much do I want in my bank account?

3. *Achievable*: Goals should be realistic and attainable. Setting overly ambitious or unattainable targets may lead to frustration and loss of motivation. It's essential to strike a balance between challenging and feasible goals.

Using the goals you listed previously, break them into achievable steps that fit your current income, time, and responsibilities.

STEPS

1. ____

2. ____

3. ____

4. ____

5. ____

4. *Relevant*: Goals should align with your values, aspirations, and long-term vision. They should be meaningful and relevant to their unique circumstances and financial situation.

LONG TERM GOALS/ FUTURE VISION

1.____

2.____

3.____

4.____

5.____

5. *Time-Bound*: Goals should have a specific time frame for completion. A deadline creates a sense of urgency and encourages consistent effort towards the objective.

TARGET DATE TO ACHIEVE GOALS:

____

STRATEGIES FOR SETTING CLEAR FINANCIAL GOALS

1. *Self-Reflection and Prioritization*: Begin by reflecting on your financial values and what prosperity and financial freedom mean to you. Identify your most important financial priorities, such as paying off debt, saving for retirement, or starting a business. Rank them in order of significance to guide your goal-setting process.

Self-Reflection and Goal Prioritization

2. *Create Long-Term and Short-Term Goals*: Divide your financial objectives into long-term (5+ years), medium-term (1-5 years), and short-term (less than 1 year) goals. This helps establish a road map and allows you to celebrate smaller victories along the way.

LONG TERM GOALS:

____

____

____

MEDIUM TERM GOALS:

____

____

____

SHORT TERM GOALS:

____

____

____

3. *Financial Health Assessment*: Assess your current financial situation, including income, expenses, debts, assets, and investments. Understanding your financial standing will help you set realistic and relevant goals.

INCOME:____

____

____

EXPENSES:____

____

____

DEBTS:____

____

____

ASSETS:____

____

____

INVESTMENTS:____

____

4. *Set Quantifiable Goals:* Ensure each goal is specific and measurable. For example, instead of saying "reduce debt," specify "pay off $5,000 credit card debt within two years."

QUANTIFIABLE GOALS:

____

____

____

____

5. *Break Goals into Actionable Steps*: Divide larger goals into smaller, actionable steps. This makes the process more manageable and less overwhelming.

ACTIONABLE STEPS:

____

____

____

____

6. *Time frame*: Set realistic deadlines for each goal, considering your financial capacity and life circumstances. Factor in unexpected events or changes that may influence your progress.

TIME FRAME:

____

____

7. *Monitor Progress Regularly*: Keep track of your financial progress. Use tools like this journal to evaluate your achievements and make necessary adjustments.

8. *Stay Flexible*: Life is unpredictable, and financial situations may change. Be open to adjusting your goals when needed but avoid deviating from them without valid reasons.

9. *Seek Professional Advice*: If needed, consult with a financial advisor or planner to receive personalized guidance on investment strategies, and financial planning.

10. *Celebrate Milestones*: Acknowledge and celebrate your achievements as you reach different milestones. This reinforcement will boost motivation and encourage continued progress.

MILESTONES:

____

____

Setting clear financial goals is a fundamental aspect of achieving prosperity and financial freedom. By adhering to the goal criteria, you can create well-defined objectives that provide direction, motivation, and financial discipline. Self-reflection, regular assessment, and flexibility are key components of a successful goal-setting process. With this clear roadmap in place, you can confidently navigate your financial journey, making informed decisions that align with your aspirations and lead to a brighter financial future.

THE ROLE OF VISUALIZATION AND POSITIVE THINKING IN ACHIEVING PROSPERITY

Visualization and positive thinking are powerful tools that can significantly impact your journey towards prosperity. By harnessing the potential of the mind and aligning it with your goals, you can unlock a wealth of opportunities and overcome obstacles on the path to success. This comprehensive exploration delves into the role of visualization and positive thinking in achieving prosperity, examining the science behind these practices and providing practical strategies for their effective implementation.

Understanding Visualization and Positive Thinking

1. *Visualization*: Visualization is a mental practice that involves creating vivid and detailed images of achieving specific goals or desired outcomes. It harnesses the brain's ability to simulate experiences, making it feel as though the envisioned scenario is real. Through visualization, you engage their senses, emotions, and thoughts to create a compelling mental picture of their prosperous future.

Follow these steps:

TAKE FIVE DEEP BREATHS: IN THROUGH THE NOSE AND OUT THROUGH THE MOUTH

VISUALIZE YOUR GOALS.

VISUALIZE YOUR IDEAL FUTURE.

2. *Positive Thinking:* Positive thinking is the practice of cultivating optimistic thoughts and beliefs. It involves focusing on the positive aspects of life, re-framing challenges as opportunities, and maintaining a hopeful outlook. By fostering positive thinking, you can increase their resilience, boost self-confidence, and enhance their overall well-being.

WRITE 5 POSITIVE THOUGHTS:

1. ____

2. ____

3. ____

4. ____

5. ____

The Science Behind Visualization/Positive Thinking

1. *Neuroplasticity*: The brain's ability to adapt and reorganize its neural connections is known as neuroplasticity. Visualization and positive thinking can harness this phenomenon by rewiring the brain towards more optimistic and goal-oriented thinking patterns. Repeatedly visualizing and affirming positive outcomes can create new neural pathways that support prosperous thinking.

2. *Reticular Activating System (RAS)*: The RAS is a network of nerves in the brain that filters incoming information. When you focus their attention on specific goals or positive thoughts, the RAS works to highlight relevant opportunities and information, increasing the likelihood of spotting resources and pathways to prosperity.

3. *Stress Reduction*: Positive thinking can reduce stress by lowering cortisol levels and promoting the release of endorphins. Reduced stress enhances cognitive function, decision-making, and problem-solving abilities, all of which are crucial for achieving prosperity.

4. *Confidence and Resilience*: Visualization and positive thinking instill a sense of confidence and resilience. Believing in your ability to achieve goals and overcome challenges builds a strong foundation for success, encouraging you to persist in their endeavors.

The Role of Visualization in Achieving Prosperity

1. *Goal Clarity and Focus*: Visualization clarifies goals and creates a clear mental picture of what prosperity looks like. It sharpens focus and enables you to align their actions with their aspirations.

2. *Motivation and Drive*: Vividly visualizing successful outcomes generates motivation and drive. The mental rehearsal of success can create an emotional connection to the desired results, encouraging you to take consistent steps towards your goals.

3. *Overcoming Limiting Beliefs*: Visualization can challenge and replace limiting beliefs that hinder prosperity. By repeatedly visualizing success, you can shift your mindset from doubt to confidence, enabling you to embrace new opportunities.

4. *Enhanced Problem-Solving*: Visualization enhances problem-solving abilities by encouraging creative thinking. When faced with challenges, individuals who have mentally rehearsed positive outcomes may approach obstacles with a more open and innovative mindset.

The Role of Positive Thinking in Achieving Prosperity

1. *Resilience in the Face of Adversity*: Positive thinking fosters resilience, helping individuals bounce back from setbacks and maintain optimism during challenging times. This unwavering optimism enables them to persevere in their pursuit of prosperity.

2. *Attracting Opportunities*: Positive thinking can attract opportunities, as people with a positive outlook are more likely to exude confidence and attract like-minded individuals who may offer support, collaboration, or beneficial connections.

3. *Empowerment and Self-Belief*: Positive thinking empowers individuals to believe in their potential and abilities. This belief in oneself can unlock the courage to take calculated risks and seize opportunities that contribute to prosperity.

4. *Improved Decision-Making*: Positive thinking enhances cognitive function, leading to better decision-making. Individuals who approach decisions with a positive mindset are more likely to make choices aligned with their long-term goals.

Practical Strategies for Visualization and Positive Thinking

1. *Create a Vision Board*: Compile images, words, and symbols that represent your prosperous future. Display the vision board in a prominent place to reinforce positive visualizations regularly.

VISION BOARD: This will take you about an hour to do. For references, use your browser and search vision boards. You will see examples and then you can create yours.

DATE VISION BOARD CREATED:

---

2. *Meditation and Guided Imagery*: Practice meditation or guided imagery sessions that focus on visualizing success and positive outcomes. Dedicate time each day to engage in these mental exercises.

Find a safe, relaxing place; get comfortable; take some deep breaths and begin imagining your success and power.

This practice works best with consistency, use the next page to track your daily meditation or visualization.

MEDITATION DAILY LOG:

3. *Positive Affirmations*: Repeat positive affirmations daily to reinforce optimistic beliefs. Over time, repetition helps interrupt negative self-talk and reinforces a more supportive mindset aligned with your goals.

Affirmations should be specific, present tense, and tailored to your goals. "I am", "I attract" are great starts.

WRITE 5 AFFIRMATIONS THAT YOU WILL REPEAT *EVERYDAY*:

1. ____

2. ____

3. ____

4. ____

5. ____

4. *Gratitude Journaling*: Maintain a gratitude journal to acknowledge and appreciate the positive aspects of your life. Reflect on your progress and visualize future achievements through journaling.

Each day, write one thing you're grateful for and one small win or sign of progress.

DAILY GRATITUDE JOURNAL:

5. *Surround Yourself with Positivity*: Surround yourself with positive influences, whether through supportive friends, mentors, or motivational content. Limit exposure to negativity that might hinder your progress.

6. *Visualization Rituals*: Incorporate visualization rituals into your daily routine. Imagine yourself succeeding in specific tasks, overcoming challenges, or achieving long-term goals.

7. *Practice Mindfulness*: Practice mindfulness to stay present and observe your thoughts. When negative thoughts arise, consciously shift your focus towards positive perspectives.

8. *Embrace Optimism*: Embrace an optimistic outlook even in the face of setbacks. See challenges as opportunities for growth and learning.

Visualization and positive thinking are potent tools that can significantly impact your journey towards prosperity. By harnessing the power of the mind and aligning thoughts with positive beliefs, you can strengthen your resilience, focus, and confidence, paving the way for a prosperous future. Embracing these practices and integrating them into daily life can lead to transformative shifts in perspective, empowering you to achieve your financial and personal aspirations with clarity, determination, and unwavering optimism.

DEVELOPING A COMPREHENSIVE FINANCIAL PLAN FOR ACHIEVING PROSPERITY

A comprehensive financial plan is a critical roadmap for achieving prosperity. It provides a structured approach to managing finances, setting and reaching financial goals, and securing a prosperous future. This in-depth guide will explore the key components of a comprehensive financial plan, step-by-step strategies for its development, and the importance of periodic review and adjustments.

Understanding the Components of a Comprehensive Financial Plan

1. *Financial Goals*: Start by defining clear, specific, and measurable financial goals. These can include short-term objectives like building an emergency fund, medium-term goals like purchasing a home, and long-term aspirations like retirement planning. Ensure that each goal aligns with your vision of prosperity.

2. *Income and Expense Management*: Assess your current income and expenses to understand your financial inflows and outflows. Create a budget that allows you to live within your means while allocating funds towards your goals.

3. *Debt Management*: Examine your existing debts, such as credit card debt, student loans, or mortgages. Develop a plan to repay debts strategically, considering interest rates and prioritizing high-interest debt.

4. *Savings and Investments*: Build a savings strategy that includes emergency savings, short-term savings, and long-term investments. Diversify investments based on your risk tolerance and time horizon for each goal.

5. *Insurance Coverage*: Evaluate your insurance needs, including health insurance, life insurance, disability insurance, and property insurance. Ensure adequate coverage to protect against unexpected events that could jeopardize your financial security.

6. *Retirement Planning*: Plan for retirement by estimating your future expenses and creating a savings plan that allows you to maintain your desired lifestyle after retiring.

7. *Estate Planning*: Consider estate planning elements like wills, trusts, and beneficiaries to ensure your assets are distributed according to your wishes and to minimize estate taxes.

8. *Tax Planning*: Strategize tax-efficient investment and retirement contributions to optimize your tax situation and maximize your savings.

9. *Risk Management*: Identify and assess potential risks that could impact your financial plan. Develop contingency plans to mitigate these risks and safeguard your financial security.

Step-by-Step Strategies for Developing a Comprehensive Financial Plan

1. *Set Financial Goals*: Determine your short-term, medium-term, and long-term financial goals. Prioritize them based on their importance and feasibility.

LONG TERM FINANCIAL GOALS:

____

____

____

MEDIUM TERM FINANCIAL GOALS:

SHORT TERM FINANCIAL GOALS:

2. *Assess Your Current Financial Situation*: Review your income, expenses, assets, debts, and insurance coverage. Understanding your current financial position will help you create a realistic plan.

Use this section to reflect on how your current finances support, or limit, your short, medium, and long-term goals.

CURRENT FINANCIAL SITUATION:

____

____

____

____

____

____

____

____

3. *Create a Budget*: Develop a budget that aligns with your financial goals. Allocate funds towards savings, debt repayment, investments, and living expenses. Outline how you plan to allocate your income.

BUDGET:_______________________________________

____

____

____

____

____

____

____

4. *Debt Repayment Strategy*: Devise a plan to pay off high-interest debts first while making consistent payments on other debts. Use this space to outline which debts you will prioritize and how you plan to pay them down.

STRATEGY FOR DEBT RELIEF:_______________________________

5. *Savings and Investment Plan:* Determine how much you need to save and invest to achieve your financial goals. Choose appropriate investment vehicles based on your risk tolerance and time horizon.

SAVINGS AND INVESTMENT PLAN: ___________________

6. *Insurance Analysis*: Evaluate your insurance needs and purchase policies that provide adequate coverage for potential risks. Use this space to note your current coverage and any gaps you may need to address.

INSURANCE:

7. *Retirement Savings Plan*: **Use this space** to estimate your retirement expenses and set a target for retirement savings. Contribute regularly to retirement accounts to achieve your retirement goals.

If retirement feels far off or unclear, use this space to record what you know now and what you want to explore further.

RETIREMENT PLAN:

____

____

____

____

____

____

____

8. *Estate Planning and Legal Documents*: Consult with an estate planning attorney to create or update essential legal documents like wills, trusts, and powers of attorney.

Use this space to note what estate planning documents you already have, what may need updating, and any questions you want to discuss with a professional.

____

____

____

____

____

____

____

____

9. *Tax Optimization*: Seek advice from a tax professional to optimize your tax situation and make informed tax-related decisions.

Use this space to note your current tax considerations, deductions or credits you may qualify for, and any questions you want to discuss with a tax professional.

____

____

____

____

____

____

____

____

THE IMPORTANCE OF PERIODIC REVIEW AND ADJUSTMENTS

1. *Life Changes*: Life is dynamic, and circumstances change. Periodically review and adjust your financial plan to accommodate life events like marriage, children, career changes, or unexpected emergencies.

2. *Market Fluctuations*: Economic conditions and investment markets fluctuate. Regularly assess your investment portfolio and consider re-balancing to align with your risk tolerance and financial goals.

3. *Goal Reassessment*: Priorities may shift over time. Reevaluate your financial goals periodically and make necessary adjustments to stay on track towards prosperity.

4. *Insurance Updates*: Review your insurance coverage regularly to ensure it meets your evolving needs. Consider adjustments in coverage as your financial situation changes.

5. *Tax Law Changes*: Tax laws can change, impacting your financial planning strategies. Stay informed about tax regulations and adjust your plan accordingly.

Developing a comprehensive financial plan is an essential step towards achieving prosperity. By addressing key components such as financial goals, income, expenses, debt, savings, investments, insurance, retirement, estate planning, and tax optimization, you can create a roadmap for financial success. Periodic review and adjustments ensure that the plan remains relevant and adaptive to life changes and economic conditions. With a well-crafted financial plan, you can navigate their financial journey with confidence, making informed decisions that align with their vision of prosperity and lead to a secure and prosperous future.

THE POWER OF HABITS AND ROUTINES IN ACHIEVING PROSPERITY

Habits and routines play a pivotal role in shaping our lives and can significantly impact our journey towards prosperity. These ingrained patterns of behavior influence how we manage our finances, pursue our goals, and respond to challenges. By harnessing the power of positive habits and well-designed routines, you can create a foundation for success, increase productivity, and achieve prosperity in various aspects of life. This comprehensive exploration delves into the science behind habits and routines, their influence on financial well-being, and practical strategies to cultivate beneficial habits and routines for prosperity.

Understanding Habits and Routines

1. *Habits*: Habits are automatic behavioral patterns acquired through repetition and reinforcement. They are deeply ingrained in our brains and occur without conscious effort. Whether good or bad, habits significantly impact our daily actions, decisions, and outcomes.

WRITE DOWN CURRENT HABITS:

____

____

____

____

current habits continued…

---

2. *Routines*: Routines are a series of activities performed in a specific order, often following a regular schedule. Routines provide structure and predictability to our lives, allowing us to manage time efficiently and focus on essential tasks.

WRITE DOWN CURRENT ROUTINE:

---

current routine continued…

____

____

____

____

____

The Science Behind Habits and Routines

1. *Neurological Basis*: Habits are formed through a process known as "neuroplasticity," which involves the strengthening of neural connections as behaviors are repeated. Over time, habits become deeply rooted in the brain, making them difficult to change.

2. *Habit Loops*: Habits follow a loop consisting of three elements: the cue, the routine, and the reward. The cue triggers the habit, the routine is the behavior itself, and the reward reinforces the habit. Understanding this loop is crucial in both breaking undesirable habits and creating beneficial ones.

3. *Conservation of Cognitive Resources*: Routines free up cognitive resources by automating repetitive tasks. By

incorporating positive habits and routines into our lives, we reduce decision fatigue and mental stress, leaving more mental energy for important decisions and creative pursuits.

The Influence of Habits and Routines on Financial Well-Being

1. *Financial Discipline*: Positive financial habits, such as regular budgeting, saving, and avoiding impulsive purchases, contribute to financial discipline. These habits lay the groundwork for building wealth and achieving prosperity.

2. *Goal Persistence*: Consistent routines help you stay focused on their financial goals. Whether it's paying off debt or investing for the future, following a structured routine enhances goal persistence.

3. *Productive Time Management*: Time-blocking and well-designed routines optimize time management. Efficiently allocating time for work, leisure, personal growth, and financial planning ensures better productivity and reduces procrastination.

4. *Stress Reduction*: Routines can alleviate financial stress by providing predictability and organization. Knowing that specific financial tasks are part of a routine reduces the anxiety associated with managing finances.

5. *Developing Healthy Financial Behaviors*: Positive habits and routines foster healthy financial behaviors, such as regular review of financial statements, monitoring investment performance, and making informed financial decisions.

Cultivating Beneficial Habits and Routines for Prosperity

1. *Identify Key Habits to Cultivate*: Reflect on your financial goals and the habits that align with achieving them. Focus on cultivating habits related to budgeting, saving, investing, and wise spending.

2. *Start Small*: Begin by introducing one new habit at a time. Starting small increases, the likelihood of success and minimizes overwhelm.

3. *Use Habit Stacking*: Associate the new habit with an existing one. For instance, link the habit of reviewing your finances with having your morning coffee or brushing your teeth.

4. *Create a Reward System*: Reinforce positive habits by rewarding yourself for consistent execution. The reward can be as simple as taking time for a hobby you enjoy or treating yourself to a small indulgence.

5. *Track Progress:* Keep a habit tracker or journal to monitor your consistency. Tracking progress provides motivation and allows you to identify areas for improvement.

6. *Commit to the Routine*: Design a daily or weekly routine that includes specific financial tasks. Dedicate time to financial planning, reviewing investments, or updating your budget.

7. *Involve an Accountability Partner*: Share your financial goals and routines with a trusted friend or family member. An accountability partner can offer support and encouragement, keeping you on track.

8. *Stay Flexible*: Be open to adjusting your routines as needed. Life changes, and adapting your routines allows you to accommodate new circumstances.

9. *Practice Mindfulness*: Stay present and intentional while performing financial tasks. Mindful execution of habits and routines enhances their effectiveness.

10. *Celebrate Milestones*: Acknowledge and celebrate your progress as you achieve financial milestones. Celebrations reinforce positive behaviors and encourage further success.

Overcoming Challenges and Breaking Negative Habits

1. *Identify Triggers*: Recognize the cues that lead to negative habits. Awareness is the first step in breaking these patterns.

2. *Replace Negative Habit*: Replace undesirable habits with positive alternatives. For example, if impulse buying is a problem, practice waiting for 24 hours before making a purchase.

3. *Seek Support*: Seek support from friends, family, or professionals if breaking negative habits proves challenging. Support systems can provide guidance and encouragement.

4. *Practice Self-Compassion*: Be compassionate towards yourself during the process of change. Overcoming long-standing habits takes time and effort.

Habits and routines have a profound influence on achieving prosperity. By understanding the science behind habits and routines, you can harness their power to build positive financial behaviors, optimize time management, and reduce stress. Cultivating beneficial habits and designing routines that align with financial goals create a foundation for success. By persistently adhering to these routines, you can achieve financial discipline, stay focused on their objectives, and ultimately pave the way for lasting prosperity in their lives.

CREATE NEW HABITS:

CREATE A NEW ROUTINE:

Routines are important part of achieving your goals. Now that you've completed this journal, it's time to start implementing all the items you've just learned about.

<u>DAILY IMPLEMENTATIONS CHECKLIST</u>:

- Focusing on your WHY.

- Remembering your motivation.

- Harnessing and powering your confidence.

- Reading your financial goals.

- Visualizing and meditation.

- Reading your positive affirmations.

- Writing down your gratitude.

This checklist is not about perfection. It's a daily reference. Use it to stay grounded, focused, and aligned with your goals. Some days you may do all of it. Some days, only one or two items. What matters is returning to it consistently.

Congratulations on taking this step and completing the workbook. You have the tools, structure, and awareness to support the life you want to build.

You are now on your way to the life you desire, *your* path to prosperity.

About The Author

TJ Hill never imagined she'd become an author. Her journey started in business consulting, where she spent years helping entrepreneurs and their teams build stronger, smoother operations. Along the way, she noticed something surprising: no matter how successful people looked on the outside, many of them felt overwhelmed when it came to managing their money.

That realization changed everything. TJ saw that what people needed wasn't complicated financial talk—they needed simple, step-by-step guidance that actually fit into real life. So she set out to create books, journals, and guides that would make money management less intimidating and far more empowering.

Her mission is simple: to help readers feel confident with their finances, take control of their money, and build the future they deserve. Through her writing, TJ shares encouragement, clarity, and a reminder that financial freedom isn't just for a few—it's possible for anyone willing to take the first step.

You can find all of her books and journals at https://tjhillbooks.com/

What's Next?

Unlock Fortune — Coming Spring 2026!